Your Everyday Legacy Poetry Devotional

By Nurse Anne

Splash impactful transformation as you go.

Intro:

Your life legacy is not just for the future, but also for everyday encounters.

As we tend to the garden of our soul and cultivate a deeper relationship with our Creator, newness and freedom will emerge. These bountiful blessings will produce joy, peace, and wonder that will refresh the lives of those we encounter.

The inward and outward transformation will spring forth with endless ripples onto the ocean of humanity.

Thanks:

God's love is infinite and all-reaching!

Mom and Dad: Amazing people who instil and radiate authenticity, strength, and altruism.

JB and Jordan: Your resolve and ingenuity are a catalyst of inspiration.

Danielle and Perry: Thanks for your example of kindness and dedication to your life passions.

Tony: Thanks for being authentic. May your memory fill hearts with smiles.

Readers and co-lifers: You are loved and cherished.

2024 By Nurse Anne

Any examples or stories are purely coincidental and not taken from any person's specific life details.

Scripture from KJV

Contents:

Your Legacy of:

1. Transformation
2. Impact
3. Kindness
4. Integrity
5. Advocacy
6. Wisdom
7. Helping Others Win
8. Truth-Telling
9. Self Worth
10. Peacemaker with Boundaries
11. Authenticity
12. Overcoming
13. Releasing Your Gifts
14. Leadership by Example and Service
15. Healing of Body, Mind, and Spirit
16. Your Faith Walk (even amidst doubts)

Psalms 145:4 - One generation shall praise thy works to another, and shall declare thy mighty acts.

Matthew 6:20-21 - But lay up for yourselves treasures in heaven, where neither moth nor rust doth corrupt, and where thieves do not break through nor steal

1. Transformation

Should I just stay the same
And never have a new name
Keep doing things the old way
Stuck in the past, afraid of a new day

OR

Find out what makes me tick.
Explore the depths of what makes me sick.
Break up the toxic soil.
Bubble up the new and let it boil.

Generational cycles and bonds of trauma
Exposed to the light will quell the drama
Discovery may erupt pain.
Uncovering shame, like thunder and rain.

This storm of discovering me.
Can rip off the shackles and make me free
So yes, this journey will be worth it.
A higher target, I will eventually hit.

Prayer, therapy, and introspection
provide epiphanies about my sense of rejection.
This inward dive into the realm of the deep
is more than baby steps, it's a forward leap.

You can begin this search in your own life as well
to sound the alarm and ring the bell.
Wake up, get up, begin the process
You're not meant to exist only under duress.

You were created for so much more.
Don't be afraid to open this door.
Your future awaits with dreams to explore.

Isaiah 43:19

Behold, I will do a new thing; now it shall spring forth; shall ye not know it? I will even make a way in the wilderness, and rivers in the desert.

No matter our age or life situation, sometimes we may feel stuck in repetitive cycles of generational patterns, unwise relationship choices, unbridled emotions, and payouts of costly mistakes.
Uncovering the sources of these patterns and doing the necessary homework to cultivate new and beneficial outcomes is possible.
Prayer, introspection, therapy, soul-searching, faith communities, self-exploration, and books and podcasts can help you navigate epiphanies of discovery and healing.
Growth and change are possible. I pray that even amidst setbacks, you will continue this worthwhile endeavor.

2. Impact

Being an example is not a small thing
Others are watching the attitude you bring
Our children, our friends, and others we know
Have a front-row seat for the stage of our show

Making a difference while you work, shop, and drive
can be an inspiration for someone to thrive
You can be the mentor that someone will need
As they follow behind, you take the lead

Discover your talents and hone a life skill
Discipline your time along with your will
The payouts render satisfaction
And infuse others with courage to jump into action

Proverbs 27:17

17 Iron sharpeneth iron; so a man sharpeneth the countenance of his friend.

Nothing that you do is small or insignificant.
You don't have to be on a stage with bright lights or have lots of followers to make an impact. Wherever you go, people are always watching to see how you react to the pressures of life. Your example of patience and emotional intelligence, along with appropriate boundaries, can make an impression that inspires your onlookers to discover new life directions.
Making a difference that benefits others starts with refining our own life trajectory.
In his book *30 Life Principles*, Dr. Charles Stanley taught that intimacy with God is the highest priority for our lives and determines our impact.

Making an Impact Tips:

- Slow down
- Be Kind
- Volunteer
- Mentor
- Role Model
- Advocate for change
- Inspire others

What else comes to your mind?

3. Kindness

You don't have to be a jerk
for your life goals to work
You can still keep it real.
While caring how others feel.

Being a mentor and providing attention.
Can even keep a student out of detention.
You could be an ordinary superhero to someone.
Causing them to rise when it's all said and done.

Speaking life can infuse people with hope.
And help them avoid numbing with dope.
You can build up a life, believe it or not.
Before you turn away, give this another thought.

It seems hard to do when others are mean.
We all have emotions, we're not a machine
Maybe the example can start with us
Responding with patience instead of a fuss

Proverbs 19:22

22 The desire of a man is his kindness: and a poor man is better than a liar.

Proverbs 15:1 reminds us that a soft and gentle answer can help diffuse situations of anger. However, this can present a challenge when rudeness and impatience get in our faces.

Taking time out of our busy schedules to rest, pray, and enjoy nature can soothe our nervous system and prepare us for the tasks ahead.

Tips for being kind:

- Be kind to yourself: Speak to yourself with compassion and avoid negative thinking. Forgive yourself for mistakes as you would others. Take care of your mental and physical health so you can be supportive of others.
- Compliment others: Pay attention to what people are saying and find opportunities to give genuine compliments.
- Practice gratitude: Make a list of things you're grateful for and put it somewhere prominent to remind yourself of the good things in your life.
- Volunteer: Volunteering can teach empathy, which can lead to more kindness.
- Start your day with kindness: In the morning, tell yourself that you'll focus on being kind and set your mind and body towards that goal.

4. Integrity

What will we do when no one can see
Think about sharing or making it all about me
Speak the whole truth or tell another lie
Whatever it takes just to get by
When we listen from Heaven, we can hear the right voice
To consider the outcome before making a choice
Does it really even matter
If I choose the former or the latter
In time you will have learned
respect can be earned
Living this way will make you stand tall
And help you avoid taking the fall
Your actions speak loud.
And will make you feel proud
Life is much better when your conscience is clear
To be bold as a lion
And not cower in fear

Proverbs 11:3

3 The integrity of the upright shall guide them: but the perverseness of transgressors shall destroy them.

Psalm 41:12

12 And as for me, thou upholdest me in mine integrity, and settest me before thy face for ever.

Proverbs 28:1 paints an interesting picture of integrity. It asks us to consider whether our actions will cause us to want to hide in shame and fear or whether we can stand tall and look others in the eye, along with our own reflections in the mirror.

- Appraise your own integrity: Consider your moral principles and ask yourself questions to identify areas for improvement.
- Define your values: Consider your personal values and the core values of your organization.
- Keep your commitments: Be trustworthy and demonstrate good follow-through.
- Be transparent: Be open, honest, and authentic in your interactions with others.
- Keep promises: Keeping promises builds trust.
- Be mindful of your behavior: Try to lead by example, be polite, respectful, and easy-going.
- Take responsibility: Understand the impact of your actions and accept responsibility for the consequences.

5. Advocacy

Sometimes in life we need help and aid
to shield us from worry and being afraid
Growing up with pain
dispels sunshine and brings the dark rain

Trauma-informed care
implores others to share
Empathy from the heart
is a great place to start

With so many in need
We can help clothe and to feed
Whether abroad or right down the street
Which of these needs will you choose to meet

Isaiah 1:17

17 Learn to do well; seek judgment, relieve the oppressed, judge the fatherless, plead for the widow.

Jeremiah 22:3

3 Thus saith the Lord; Execute ye judgment and righteousness, and deliver the spoiled out of the hand of the oppressor: and do no wrong, do no violence to the stranger, the fatherless, nor the widow, neither shed innocent blood in this place.

Is there a cause that tugs at your heart?

Do you sometimes wonder if you can even make a difference?
What is even a tiny thing you believe could help as you go about your life duties?

Here are some tips for being an advocate, whether it's for yourself or for a cause:

- Be prepared: Know your rights and the issue you're advocating for. You can research online, but you should also check the accuracy of your information by looking at multiple sources.
- Communicate effectively: Be clear, concise, and persuasive. Structure your message to fit the situation and your audience.
- Be confident: Believe in yourself and your abilities. Confidence can help you take risks and try new things.
- Be polite: Remember names and thank people who help you.
- Be a good listener: Be supportive and build relationships.
- Follow up: Maintain good records and request things in writing. Follow up with legislators and their staff.

6. Wisdom

Don't be a fool
just so you can look cool
The way of the wise
helps you to rise
Sometimes it's not fun
But the work has to get done
You don't have to wonder or even to guess
Follow the clear path or your life will be a mess
When you seek after God's mind
revelations will unwind
You can find the answers all in the Book
Just open it up and take a long look

James 1:5

5 If any of you lack wisdom, let him ask of God, that giveth to all men liberally, and upbraideth not; and it shall be given him.

Matthew 7:24

24 Therefore whosoever heareth these sayings of mine, and doeth them, I will liken him unto a wise man, which built his house upon a rock:

Sometimes, a fear of missing out on all the glitter around us can cause spiritual blindness towards something genuinely satisfying.
Searching for wisdom can involve listening to elders and others who strive to make better choices.
Just as Proverbs 3 advises, when we learn from and listen to God instead of relying on our limited insight, we can be guided toward better scenarios for ourselves and those we care for.

Here are some tips for developing wisdom:

> Be compassionate and empathetic
> Try to see things from other people's perspectives, and listen to them. This can help you become more open-minded and conscientious, which can impact your decisions. It can also help you understand your own feelings and emotions, and how to control them.
> Ask questions
> Asking thoughtful, open-ended questions can help you learn information you didn't know you needed.
> Rest
> Research shows that when you're resting, your brain is actually busier than when you're concentrating on a task. Resting is a time when you can replay conversations and situations from the day.

7. Helping Others Win

Are you willing to invest

To help someone be their best

What skill can you teach

Can you provide some outreach

The reward is for both

when you fuel someone's growth

Allowing another to succeed

will meet their great need

along with the sense of pride

you will see doors open wide

Matthew 5:16

16 Let your light so shine before men, that they may see your good works, and glorify your Father which is in heaven.

One of life's greatest joys is helping another succeed. Even if you don't have a lot of time to officially coach or mentor, as you go about your responsibilities at work, school, and or the community, it's nice to sprinkle in eye contact, listening, and smiles.

Here are some ways to help others win:

Volunteer

Volunteering can be a win-win for both you and those in need. You can meet new people, enrich yourself, and even improve your health.

Donate unused items

Give coaching feedback

Feedback can help people understand what they are doing well and what they need to improve. It can also help them align their goals with your expectations.

Make people feel important

You can make people feel important by smiling, remembering their names, praising them, and making an effort to learn about their interests.

Practice kindness

Acts of kindness can make both the giver and recipient feel good, and they can help create positive communities.

8. Truth-Telling

When you open your mouth
does everything go south
Or do you choose what you say
to brighten someone's day

We need your unique voice
in this world full of choice
So come on, let it out
Release your perspective along with a shout

We can filter our speech in order to be wise
instead of being harsh to cut down to size
Is it true? Is it kind?
Will it lead another to an elevated state of mind

3 John 4

4 I have no greater joy than to hear that my children walk in truth.

Psalm 51:6

6 Behold, thou desirest truth in the inward parts: and in the hidden part thou shalt make me to know wisdom.

Are you a truth-teller or a people-pleaser? Of course, wisdom reminds us to pause before speaking to ensure kindness and consider the other person's feelings.

It can be hard to wait in the heat of an angry exchange, but stopping to think about the big picture can help us formulate a better reply.

Proverbs 15:23 provides an exciting guide for our verbal responses. We are reminded that making an apt answer, one appropriate or suitable in the circumstances, can bring joy to both parties and emphasize the value of speaking the right thing at the right time. At the same time, it's vital to convey truth and value filtered through emotional intelligence.

Speaking your truth can be challenging, but it can also be a source of strength. Here are some tips that may help:

> Be intentional: Identify your values and what they mean to you.

> Consider your audience: Customize your words to the person and the situation.

> Be honest and non-confrontational: Present your truth in a way that's non-charged and respectful.

> Be open to feedback: Listen and respond rather than react.

> Be mindful of timing: It might be appropriate to pause and speak later.

> Let go of expectations: Don't get stuck on the outcome.

9. Self Worth

You are enough they tell me to claim

It's hard to believe when I ponder my shame

When I look in the mirror, myself is who I blame

Lord, help me to see the treasure you made

You showed me my worth by the great price that you paid

Don't allow the thief to steal, kill, and destroy

Ultimately, You provide a real sense of joy

Hebrews 10:35

35 Cast not away therefore your confidence, which hath great recompence of reward.

A healthy sense of self-worth does not always come naturally.

Healing from trauma bonds and criticism imposed by others is one way to start the journey. Even after doing our self-esteem homework, our minds can tempt us to replay the broken records of the past.

Cultivating our sense of self-worth will help with the inner confidence to radiate impact and blessings on the lives of others.

Refining our values and integrity can foster our sense of self-respect and confidence.

Here are some tips that may help improve your self-worth:

- Be kind to yourself: Challenge negative thoughts about yourself, say positive things to yourself, and do something nice for yourself every day. You can also try practicing self-compassion.
- Recognize your strengths: Celebrate your successes, accept compliments, and make a note of them to look back on when you're feeling down. You can also write down a list of things you admire about yourself.
- Set boundaries: Avoid being a people pleaser, and remember that it's okay to say no.
- Take care of yourself: Take care of your body, reconnect with things you're passionate about, and engage in work that's exciting and fulfilling. You can also try taking up a hobby, being creative, or volunteering.

10. Peacemaker with Boundaries

Do I have to go first when you're feeling
your worst
the fight that we had
makes both of us sad

How can we make things right
and avoid this misunderstood fight
We both played a part
let's show love from the heart

Let's not repeat this mistake
Uncover the root and reveal what's at stake
Respect is at the core
for our friendship to not be a chore

Let's work this out and move on from the
past
putting in the right effort can make all of this
last.

Matthew 5:9

9 Blessed are the peacemakers: for they shall be called the children of God.

Romans 14:19

19 Let us therefore follow after the things which make for peace, and things wherewith one may edify another.

Being a peacemaker is a beautiful thing. At the same time, you don't have to be a doormat and feel walked on. Even though humility is critical, sometimes the prescription for change can call for some time away and introspection.

Searching our hearts and accepting constructive feedback can lay the groundwork for both parties to flourish.

Here are some tips for setting boundaries during an argument:

Set boundaries early
It's easier to set boundaries at the beginning of a relationship than to try to change things later.

Be clear and concise
When you communicate your boundaries, be honest and clear about what you need and what you're willing to tolerate.

Be firm but dispassionate
Try to stay calm and respectful, and avoid apologizing or explaining.

Establish consequences
Be clear about what will happen if your boundaries are crossed, such as ending a relationship or taking a break.

Consider your limits
Know your limits and set boundaries around what's appropriate for emotionally charged conversations.

11. Authenticity

Do I have to be fake

for your acceptance to take

Is it possible to be real

and tell you how I feel.

I have my perspective

That will meet my objective

I also value your authenticity

it charges our relationship with electricity

Show your true self

Don't place your gifts on the shelf

It's a beautiful thing

when you let your soul sing!

Proverbs 4:23

23 Keep thy heart with all diligence; for out of it are the issues of life.

Philippians 4:8

8 Finally, brethren, whatsoever things are true, whatsoever things are honest, whatsoever things are just, whatsoever things are pure, whatsoever things are lovely, whatsoever things are of good report; if there be any virtue, and if there be any praise, think on these things.

Genuine authenticity grounded in solid values energizes you and those you encounter. Guided by emotional intelligence to know the appropriate situations and timelines to unleash full disclosure will set the pace.

Overcoming fear and worry about what others think is a major milestone for this trajectory.

Depending on the environment and social situation, this can sometimes be difficult. Still, I assure you it is definitely worth the payouts of an unhindered life story that you present to the world.

Authenticity is when your internal sense of self matches your outward behavior. Here are some tips to be more authentic:

Celebrate authenticity
Research suggests that people feel more well-being when they feel like they're living their values and perspectives.

Speak your truth
Being honest and transparent about your thoughts and emotions can show others that you're responsible and trustworthy.

Embrace vulnerability
Authentic speaking can lead to deeper connections and more meaningful communication.

Live your values
Make a list of your values and rank them in order of importance. Let these values guide your choices and decisions.

Face your fears
Don't let stories you tell yourself get in the way of what you want to do.

Accept feedback

12. Overcoming

Don't let your habit make you a slave

With help from the Lord you don't have to cave

It's possible to change

Your life vision to rearrange

Even though the effort seems like a chore

this life you create holds so much in store

Do what you have to do

make it to the prize and see this through

1 John 5:4

4 For whatsoever is born of God overcometh the world: and this is the victory that overcometh the world, even our faith.

Philippians 4:13

I can do all things through Christ who strengtheneth me.

What are you trying to overcome? Is it possible, even if that means starting today, to conquer compulsions, habits, addictions, generational cycles, and thought strongholds? This can be your legacy, not just for the future but in your current situation, to improve the life of yourself and those you love.

We know this war is not just physical but mental and spiritual, and it can even seem mystical. Thankfully, God provided Heavenly armor to assist us overcome destructive forces.

Here are some tips that may help you overcome challenges:

- Make a plan: Plan ahead, even though you can't know what the future holds.
- Ask for help: Asking for help is a strength and can help you learn and overcome problems.
- Feel your feelings: Don't mask your feelings, as they can become trapped energy and have negative health consequences if ignored. Meditation can help you feel your feelings.
- Practice mindfulness: Mindfulness can help you accept things as they are and counteract worrying and rumination. It may also help reduce symptoms of depression in some people.
- Challenge negative thoughts: Remind yourself that your thoughts aren't facts and try to reframe them in a more positive way.

- Exercise: Exercise can improve your mood, outlook on life, and mental wellness.
- Help others: Helping others can make you feel good and reinforce feelings of optimism.
- Try relaxation techniques: Relaxation exercises can help with anxiety and help you fall asleep.
- Practice diaphragmatic breathing: Deep breathing can improve your attention levels and emotional well-being.

Here are some tips that may help you achieve success in life:

Set clear goals
This can help you focus on what's important, see the bigger picture, and stay motivated.
Believe in yourself
Having faith in your abilities can help you keep pushing through and avoid giving up before reaching your goals.
Remove distractions
Make a list of things that distract you, like your phone, TV, or stressful people, and try to change your habits so you can focus on success.
Develop a growth mindset
This can help you approach challenges with a positive attitude and find ways to overcome them.
Keep learning

Try to learn something new every day, whether it's in your personal or professional life.

13. Releasing Your Gifts

What lights your fire and makes you inspired

Does it keep you up at night crafting it just right

I'm excited to see how awesome it must be

Don't hoard your gifts just for you. Let them loose for the world to view

2 Timothy 1:6

6 Wherefore I put thee in remembrance that thou stir up the gift of God, which is in thee by the putting on of my hands.

Proverbs 18:16

16 A man's gift maketh room for him, and bringeth him before great men.

What is your creative passion? With so many choices, sometimes we have multiple loves. Cooking, writing, drawing, poetry, singing, dancing, volunteering, creating content, and so many more are some items that could be on your list. I've learned that if we dig into and discover what we were passionate about even in childhood, it can be our natural gift that we are excited to refine. Even amid busy schedules, we can chip away at our life passions and gifts a little at a time. It helps us bypass quick dopamine fixes that sometimes lead us the wrong way. Working on our life passions and releasing them to others provides more sustainable satisfaction and healthier dopamine.

So...Go for it!

Here are some tips to help you discover your gifts:

Reflect on your past
Consider what you enjoyed doing as a child, what you're passionate about now, and what's important to you. You can also think about any childhood talents or interests you had.

Consider your present
Pay attention to activities that make you feel at ease, and think about what you're good at with little effort. You can also consider any compliments you receive.

Ask others
Ask friends and family for their input, or consider what others associate with you.

Take action
Try something new, and put your gifts into practice. The more you use your gifts, the stronger they'll become.

14. Leadership by Example and Service

It's not just my job, we work as a team

Helping each other, even though difficult it might seem.

All contributions are welcome during this task

even much better when no one has to ask.

When we display humility, it greatly inspires

causing our vision to reach even higher

We all learn from each other

and can bond like sisters and brothers

Psalm 78:72

72 So he fed them according to the integrity of his heart; and guided them by the skilfulness of his hands.

Proverbs 11:14

14 Where no counsel is, the people fall: but in the multitude of counsellors there is safety.

Do you find it refreshing when your leader helps everyone out? In addition, when they listen as much as they give commands, show a genuine interest in their teammates, and practice empathy, humility, and kindness.

Here are some tips for being a servant leader:

Empathy
Understand how others feel and respond appropriately to their emotions. This can help you understand your team and why they feel a certain way.

Active listening
Pay attention to what others are saying without interrupting, judging, or imposing your own agenda. Ask open-ended questions, paraphrase, reflect, and summarize what you hear.

Awareness
Knowledge can help you understand issues involving ethics, power, and values. This can help you view situations from a more holistic perspective.

Commitment to growth
Take a personal interest in the ideas and suggestions from everyone, and encourage employee involvement by sharing power and decision-making.

Conceptualization

Imagine the possibilities of the future and reconcile it with current realities. This can help you visualize a bright future and take the necessary steps to get there.

Healing

Support and heal your followers by addressing issues or conflicts within the team or organization. This can lead to a more supportive and collaborative work environment, improving employee morale and job satisfaction

Here are some tips for being a humble leader:

Ask for help

Asking for help can help you maintain a healthy work-life balance and shows that you don't pretend to know everything. You can ask a mentor or coach for help, or share challenges with your team.

Seek feedback

Being open to feedback from your colleagues shows that you're willing to learn and improve. It can also help create a culture where it's safe to fail and grow.

Admit your mistakes

Admitting your mistakes can strengthen your relationships with your team and show that you're human. You can also learn from your mistakes to develop better techniques for achieving your goals.

Ask questions

Ask open-ended questions that you don't already know the answer to, such as questions that start with "how" or "what".

Accept feedback

Be open to constructive criticism and use it as an opportunity for growth. Accepting feedback shows that you value your team's input and the importance of collaboration.

Acknowledge mistakes

Learning from your mistakes can help you lead by example and show your team that mistakes can be useful.

15. Healing of Body, Mind, and Spirit

Take care of your health
because it's your wealth

Healthy foods and drinking water too
are some of the tips, just to name a few

Reduce mental stress
so you can be at your best

Connect with the Lord in a quiet space
sometimes on your knees or even your face

Body, mind, and spirit work together in synergy
Giving you the best chance to have abundant energy!

3 John 2

2 Beloved, I wish above all things that thou mayest prosper and be in health, even as thy soul prospereth.

What tops the list of your most significant investments?
When we pour into our health of body, mind, and spirit, we can reap bountiful dividends.
Sticking to proper nutrition, stretching and exercise, working on our mental clarity, and spending time with our heavenly Father is an A+ prescription for an abundant life.

Here are some tips for living a healthy lifestyle:

Eat healthy
A balanced diet can help you maintain a healthy weight, reduce your risk of chronic diseases, and stay energized. Fruits are a key part of a healthy diet, as they contain many nutrients your body needs.
Exercise
Exercise can help build fitness levels, reduce the risk of serious illnesses, improve mental health, relieve stress, and strengthen your immune system.
Get enough sleep
Quality sleep can give you the energy you need to exercise, do chores, and socialize.
Stay hydrated
Drinking water helps with digestion, nutrient circulation, and keeping your skin healthy.
Reduce stress.
Practice gratitude.

16. Your Faith-Walk

(even amidst doubts)

The pressures around
try to push my faith walk back down
but I can press on to believe
Working for trust to achieve
Such great treasures we find
When we seek after His mind

Hebrews 11:1

11 Now faith is the substance of things hoped for, the evidence of things not seen.

Here are some tips for a faith walk:

Pray

Prayer can help you establish a deeper trust with God and invite Him into your life. You can try praying without ceasing, giving thanks in all circumstances, and praying before meals. You can also try scheduling time for prayer, joining a prayer group, or committing to praying with a significant other or roommate.

Read the Bible

Reading the Bible can help you practice your faith, even if you aren't at church. You can try taking your Bible with you outside to read and get some fresh air. You can also try participating in small group Bible study sessions.

Meditate

Meditation can help you improve your self-awareness, ease stress, and settle nervous thoughts and emotions. You can try meditating in the morning for at least 10 minutes.

Forgive

Unforgiveness can make your spirit feeble, prayers ineffective, and your faith weak. You can try deciding to forgive anyone you haven't yet, and to forgive immediately in the future.

Examine yourself

You can try examining yourself to see if you are living in accordance with your faith, and make adjustments as the Lord leads you.

Have an eternal perspective

Walking by faith means fixing your eyes on what is eternal, rather than what is seen.

Thanks for hanging out and enjoying this poetry devotional!

Please share this with others.

For more inspirational wellness and CrEaTiVe Entertainment with a purpose see you at

NURSEANNE.COM

Discover more exciting and soul-enriching titles by Nurse Anne:

Help Each Other Heal

Poetry Devotional

By Nurse Anne

With excerpts for mutual healing from my favorite collections.

Intro: Healing of body, mind, and spirit is more readily achieved with the mutual help of one another. May we all go forth planting and

watering kindness, love, empathy,

and compassion for ourselves, our

loved ones, and those we encounter

along our path.

Ignite Life

Poetry Devotional

By Nurse Anne

Spill your passion to ignite healing and blessings for all!

"As you go" dare to inspire and bless everyone in your path.

The life stories we encounter daily are filled with struggle, triumph, joy, sorrow, self-doubt, and everything in between.

Challenge yourself to discover these stories and ignite passion and potential for your own journey along with mutual encouragement for others.

As a certified emergency and mental health registered nurse on the frontlines for over 30 years and still going, I am continually learning humanity on every level. Our individual experiences collide to weave a patchwork of beauty and grace.

Mental Healing
Poetry Devotional

Inviting you to investigate and embrace God's promise of power, love, and a sound mind.

By Nurse Anne

Presenting my original spoken word pieces in this devotional.

Life challenges are discussed, along with God-ordained courage and healing to help us turn away from mindsets controlled by fear. Inspiration to step into our true destiny of a faith walk and purpose-driven path.

Inspiration

Battles

Devotional

By Nurse Anne

Biblical Medicine for Real Life

Biblical Medicine for Real Life. Soul-searching with a dose of encouragement!

The battle to stay inspired can seem overwhelming at times. Yet, God reminds us that our faith should not be in the power of people but in His wisdom. Fear not, as you embark on this journey of allowing the Lord to search your life. Let the Holy Spirit's spotlight penetrate your heart, mind, will, emotions, your everything. Whatever might seem difficult for the moment will yield a reward of peace and purpose.

Find new hope and inspiration on this A to Z devotional exploration.

WORD

PUzZLeS

Devotional

Wisdom and Biblical Rx inspired by the Ultimate Wordsmith.

By Nurse Anne

Interesting words linked to everyday life drama, & our inner thought struggles, then paired with relevant Biblical prescriptions. Get your dose. Overcome and thrive.

WORD PUzZLeS A-Z
From Nurseanne.com
Ministry to Inspire, Advocate, Encourage, Create.
Certified Emergency and Mental Health RN.

Encouragement, hope, and new light for your life journey. Unique words along with inspirational wellness and Biblical prescriptions. Medicine for your soul.

Energized Health

Body, Mind and Spirit

Lifestyle Devotional

By Nurse Anne

Inspirational Wellness along with Biblical prescriptions to develop a mind at peace and to cultivate your walk with God. Also, health tips designed to jumpstart your energized life of purpose.

Nurse Anne is a certified emergency and mental health registered nurse of 30 years and still going. Enjoy this devotional designed to propel your total health for body, mind, & spirit.

Let's get started!

Mental Strength

Devotional

By Nurse Anne

31 days of focus for growing your mental wellness and resilience.

Deepen your roots of mental resilience along with building your faith on solid ground with this life-enhancing devotional. Your mental wellness can blossom and thrive for your exponential growth.

Psalm 1:3 And he shall be like a tree planted by the rivers of water, that bringeth forth his fruit in his season; his leaf also shall not wither; and whatsoever he doeth shall prosper.

The Mental Files

First 6 Stories Edition

--- Sheep Among Wolves

--- Dr. John Doe

--- A Tent Under the Bridge

--- Defenders of the Weak

--- Ready, Willing and Able

--- Out Of Control

By Nurse Anne

Also now available as an

Exciting Audiobook!!

Audible and iTunes

Ride along with the frontline workers as they try to rescue those in crisis. Mental, physical and spiritual. Thought and memory disorders, disabilities, homelessness, addictions, despair, bullying, and more inspiration battles. Not to mention the inner thought strongholds and relationship drama of the workers.

What role does God play in the outcome?

The shifts are 24/7. Buckle up for the compelling drama series filled with danger, action, suspense, romance, faith and inspiration.

The Mental Files:

Book 1: Sheep Among Wolves - intro

Ride along with officer Leon and caseworker Lita as they try to convince the man hovered on the edge of the bridge not to do the unthinkable?

And will the naive young lady with the unexpected test result whose mind is being ravaged by frightening hallucinations trust the frontline workers? Or will she listen to her so-called boyfriend that she met at the bus stop? If only the little lamb knew the dangerous plans the street predator had in mind for her.

Will the lonely caseworker fall for the handsome officer in spite of the nagging red flags? Will she rely on her faith or go with her feelings?

Will the young man caught in the web of crime find a way out?

Ride along on the journey as the drama continues in the next story.

The Mental Files: Dr. John Doe

Why was the gray-haired man with a confused look running in and out of traffic screaming that he was a doctor? Follow Officer Leon, caseworker Lita, the nurses, and their newest ride along on the adventure from the street to the healthcare system. Can they figure out who the mystery man really is? And what about the young man who just narrowly escaped a life of crime? Will his negative thoughts pull him down further and place his loved ones in danger? Or can he find inspiration to pursue a better life?

Will the caseworker and officer take their relationship to the next level? Thought battles and memory struggles rage in this ongoing drama.

Continue the adventure in the next story.

The Mental Files: A Tent Under The Bridge

Why does Abigail continue to live under the bridge? Will she allow the frontline workers to help her find a safer and healthier life? Will her long-lost mystery daughter be able to forgive her? Or will Abigail's choices place her daughter in further danger?

Ride along with Mars on his first paramedic shifts. Can he handle the intense trauma and drama? Will the handsome officer ask his big question to the beautiful caseworker? Or will his buddies convince him he will never change and would be making a mistake?

Join the frontline workers as they continue rescue efforts for the minds and lives of the vulnerable.

The story continues.

The Mental Files: Defenders of the Weak

Can Chandra break out of her paralyzing fear and anxiety? Stop allowing the bullies to take over her existence and place her in danger? Will she be able to help the stranger with a similar struggle? Or will the opposition take them both down?

Will the frontline worker's project to help the less fortunate be thwarted by the community and church members who don't want their comfort disturbed?

Is the opposition willing to place others in danger to keep their status quo?

Strongholds to be broken. A God who is able.

The shifts are 24/7. Buckle up as the bumpy ride continues.

The Mental Files: Ready, Willing, and Able

Ride along with the frontline workers on the continuing drama as they discover that problems exist in every type of household. For richer or poorer. And sometimes, the unlikeliest of people can be the actual heroes. Abilities triumph over a spectrum of doubt.

Will the young paramedic make wise or hasty relationship decisions? Why does the mental health nurse get sent to the ER? Can the community and church finally accept the so-called different people in their midst?

Leading you into the action with the season finale.

The Mental Files: Out Of Control

Season Finale

One more won't hurt. When does the seemingly harmless fun cross into the realm of out of control? Placing others in danger.
Does the entitled patient comply with his treatment? Or will he make the frontline workers pay?
Will the big event get canceled due to the officer's mistake? Can he be forgiven? Given the benefit of the doubt?
What will reign? New beginnings or old habits?

Get ready to be a part of the adventure, advocacy, awareness, and action!

For more Inspirational

Wellness and

CrEaTiVe Entertainment

With a Purpose see you at

NURSEANNE.COM

Be Blessed

Made in the USA
Columbia, SC
04 April 2025